2012

JUL

SNORKELING

FOR FUN!

By Jessica Gunderson

Content Advisers: Jason Bennis, Marine Program Manager, Sun Coast Regional Office,
National Parks Conservation Association, Hollywood, Florida
Rachel Wilborn, Marine Biologist, Florida Fish and Wildlife Conservation Commission, Miami, Florida
Reading Adviser: Susan Kesselring, M.A., Literacy Educator, Rosemount-Apple Valley-Eagan (Minnesota) School District

Compass Point Books ✦ Minneapolis, Minnesota

Compass Point Books
151 Good Counsel Drive
P.O. Box 669
Mankato, MN 56002-0669

This book was manufactured with paper containing at least 10 percent post-consumer waste.

Photographs ©: Bob Krist/Corbis, front cover (left); Gert Johannes Jacobus Vrey/Shutterstock, front cover (right), back cover; Dan Burton/Nature Picture Library, 4; Norbert Wu/Minden Pictures, 5; North Wind Picture Archives, 6; topal/Shutterstock, 7; VK/Shutterstock, 8; DJ Mattaar/Shutterstock, 9; Wolfgang Amri/Shutterstock, 10; Photodisc, 11; Brett Stoltz/Shutterstock, 12 (top); alle/Shutterstock, 12 (bottom); Dario Sabljak/Shutterstock, 13 (top); Courtesy of Oceanic Worldwide, 13 (middle); Karon Dubke/Capstone Press, 13 (bottom), 16, 17; Diane N. Ennis/Shutterstock, 14; Martin Valigursky/Shutterstock, 15; Catherine Ledner/Riser/Getty Images, 18-19; Gina Smith/Shutterstock, 20; Suzanne Tucker/Shutterstock, 21; Vasko Miokovic/iStockphoto, 22; Geoffrey Hudson/iStockphoto, 23; Specta/Shutterstock, 24; javarman/Shutterstock, 25; Nick Poling/Shutterstock, 26; Dr. David Wachenfeld/Auscape/Minden Pictures, 27 (left); Karoline Cullen/Shutterstock, 27 (right); Galina Barskaya/Shutterstock, 28; Marek Cech/Shutterstock, 29; Dmitry Ersler/Shutterstock, 31, 47; Steven Coling/Shutterstock, 32; Maxime Bilodeau/Shutterstock, 33; Michael Ledray/Shutterstock, 34; Franck Camhi/Shutterstock, 35; Corbis/Royalty-Free, 36; Harald Bolten/iStockphoto, 37; Flip Nicklin/Minden Pictures, 38; Wayne Johnson/Shutterstock, 39; AP Images, 40; Patrick Ward/Corbis, 41; HIP/Art Resource, NY, 42 (left); Popperfoto/Getty Images, 42 (right); Bettmann/Corbis, 43 (left); NOAA/PRNewsFoto/Newscom, 43 (right); Alexey Stiop/Shutterstock, 44; Zang Lei/Photocome/Newscom, 45.

Editor: Brenda Haugen
Page Production: Heidi Thompson
Photo Researcher: Marcie Spence
Art Director: LuAnn Ascheman-Adams
Creative Director: Joe Ewest
Editorial Director: Nick Healy
Managing Editor: Catherine Neitge

Library of Congress Cataloging-in-Publication Data
Gunderson, Jessica.
  Snorkeling for fun! / by Jessica Gunderson.
     p. cm. — (For Fun!)
  Includes index.
  ISBN 978-0-7565-4034-0 (library binding)
1. Skin diving—Juvenile literature. I. Title. II. Series.

GV838.672.G86 2009
797.2'3—dc22   2008037571

Visit Compass Point Books on the Internet at www.compasspointbooks.com
or e-mail your request to custserv@compasspointbooks.com

Table of Contents

The Basics

INTRODUCTION / Adventures in Snorkeling. 4

HISTORY / Early Exploring 6

TYPES OF DIVING / Snorkel or Scuba. 8

UNDERWATER LIFE / What to See in the Sea. 10

BASIC EQUIPMENT / The Bare Necessities. 12

Doing It

HOW TO SNORKEL / By Land or By Sea. 14

SNORKELING GEAR / Mask and Snorkel 16

SNORKELING ATTIRE / Suit Up. 18

GETTING WET / Take the First Plunge 20

SAFETY / Rules to Snorkel By. 22

PLANTS AND ANIMALS / Under the Sea 24

DANGEROUS CREATURES / Look, But Don't Touch 26

IMPORTANT ITEMS / Think Ahead 28

ON THE SHORE / Maintaining Your Equipment 30

People, Places, and Fun

AROUND THE WORLD / The Great Barrier Reef 32

CONSERVATION / Clean Water 34

SHARKS / Fear of the Fin 36

TOP SNORKELING SPOTS / Where to Go 38

NOTABLE PEOPLE / Making It Happen. 40

• •

TIMELINE / What Happened When?. 42

TRIVIA / Fun Snorkeling Facts 44

QUICK REFERENCE GUIDE / Snorkeling Words to Know 46

GLOSSARY / Other Words to Know 47

WHERE TO LEARN MORE 47

INDEX 48

Note: In this book, there are two kinds of vocabulary words. Snorkeling Words to Know are words specific to snorkeling. They are defined on page 46. Other Words to Know are helpful words that are not related only to snorkeling. They are defined on page 47.

Adventures in Snorkeling

Have you ever gazed at the ocean and wondered what lives beneath its waves? Have you ever wanted to see schools of tropical fish, underwater plants, and maybe even a shark or two?

Snorkeling is a way to see underwater creatures up close. A whole world exists in the earth's oceans. Colorful fish chase each other through mazes of coral reefs. Seaweed sways in the ocean waves. Sharks and whales swallow dozens of fish in one giant gulp.

Snorkelers can watch underwater creatures in their natural setting. This amazing world is yours to discover. Get ready for the great adventure of snorkeling!

Early Exploring

In ancient times, kings and other rulers sent men to explore under water. Explorers dove into the seas to find ways to fend off approaching enemies. These explorers could stay under water only a short time, though. Soon people began inventing devices to help them breathe under water.

One design was a leather hood with a breathing bag attached. The bag was made from a sheep's bladder. But the design had problems. Water pressure folded the bag.

Sixteenth-century woodcut of an underwater diver and a soldier.

In 1819, Augustus Siebe, a German artillery officer, created a diving helmet (left). A hose was connected to the helmet. Air was pumped from the surface into the helmet. In the early 1900s, ocean exploration became an important scientific field. Scientists developed new ways to draw in air while submerged in water. Soon snorkeling became popular as a sport as well as for scientific and military explorations.

Snorkel or Scuba

Snorkeling is swimming along the surface of the water while wearing a mask and a snorkel. The mask allows the snorkeler to see under water. The snorkel is a tube that extends above the surface of the water. It lets the snorkeler breathe while his or her face is in the water.

Snorkeling

Scuba diving

Scuba diving is different from snorkeling. Scuba divers wear masks, buoyancy control devices that allow them to stay under water, and tanks full of air. They breathe through hoses that are connected to the tanks. Scuba divers can dive down into the ocean's depths. They don't have to stay near the surface to breathe. Special training is needed to scuba dive.

An experienced snorkeler also can do what is called free diving. When free diving, he or she takes a huge breath of air and dives deep into the water. The free diver must return to the surface before his or her air runs out. Beginning snorkelers should never try to free dive.

What to See in the Sea

Snorkeling is more than just swimming for fun. People snorkel to see underwater life and to marvel at the wonders of the ocean.

More than 80 percent of all life on Earth lives beneath the ocean's surface. A large number of these life forms live in and around coral reefs. These large, underwater structures are made from tiny creatures called coral polyps. Coral reefs are beautiful and alive with activity. This makes them popular snorkeling sites.

When you venture under water, you will see many plants and animals. Some common marine plants are algae and sea grass. You also will see many colorful fish, such as angelfish and cowfish. Sea turtles and sea snakes may glide past you through the water. Dolphins may jump and dive in the distance. You might even catch a glimpse of a shark!

Blue-spotted Ribbontail Ray
The blue-spotted ribbontail ray lives among coral reefs. But don't touch him! He's venomous.

The Bare Necessities

Not a lot of training is needed to snorkel, but you must know how to swim. You will also need some basic equipment. You can rent snorkeling gear from local shops, or you can buy your own.

Mask: The mask is the most important piece of snorkeling gear. The mask fits around your eyes and nose and has a window in front of your eyes. Through the window you can see the treasures of the underwater world.

Snorkel: The snorkel is the tube you breathe through. It can be attached to your mask. The snorkel mouthpiece fits inside your mouth, and the tube curves in a J-shape around your head. The shape of the snorkel allows you to breathe while you are floating facedown in the water.

Swim fins: Fins attached to your feet help you move through the water quickly and easily. Swim fins are made of flexible rubber. They fit like shoes and are flat like a fish's fin.

Snorkel vest: A snorkel vest goes on over your head and is worn on your chest. The vest is held in place by straps that wrap around your back and between your legs. You fill the vest by blowing air into it with your mouth. Use a snorkel vest if you're not a good swimmer or if you're snorkeling far from the shore. Resorts, cruise lines, and some snorkel boats require the use of a snorkel vest.

Wet suit: Many snorkelers wear wet suits. Wet suits are tight-fitting and are made from flexible, stretchy material. Wet suits keep the snorkeler warm and provide protection from cuts, scrapes, and stings.

By Land or By Sea

People of all ages can snorkel and explore the underwater world. Snorkeling can be done in nearly any body of water. Snorkelers explore both saltwater, such as oceans, seas, and gulfs, and freshwater, such as lakes, rivers, and streams.

There are two ways to snorkel: either from the shore or from a boat. In shore snorkeling, you enter the water from the shore or beach. You put on your snorkeling gear while on land and then wade into the water. Local dive shops can tell you the best places to shore snorkel.

Boat snorkeling also is a popular way to enjoy the sport. Tour boats take snorkelers out to sea. You put on your gear while on the boat. Then you enter the water. When you're finished, you swim back to the boat, and the captain takes you back to shore.

Mask and Snorkel

Whether you decide to rent or buy your gear, make sure it fits. A poorly fitting mask will let in too much water and will ruin your snorkeling fun.

To check if the mask fits correctly, hold it in front of your face without attaching the strap. Settle the mask so it rests comfortably around your eyes and nose. Slowly inhale through your nose. The mask should stay in

place, even when you take your hand away. If it doesn't, search for another mask.

Choosing the right snorkel is also important. The mouthpiece of the snorkel should fit comfortably in your mouth. You should be able to get a good, deep breath through the tube.

Suit Up

The wet suit you choose depends on the type of snorkeling you will be doing. Even if you are snorkeling in warm, tropical waters, you may want to get a wet suit. Water can be colder than you expect. Your swim won't be much fun if you are cold. Wet suits also protect from sunburn, stings, and cuts.

Two popular types of snorkeling wet suits are dive skins and traditional wet suits. Dive skins

Wet suits

fit close to your body. They are made from Lycra, an elastic nylon fabric. Dive skins don't provide much warmth, so they are only used in warm water.

Traditional wet suits are worn in colder waters. They are made from insulated material and are lined with nylon. Wet suits allow a layer of water to leak in next to your skin. This water is heated by your body and helps keep you warm.

Take the First Plunge

Your first time snorkeling is exciting, but it also may be a bit scary. Before you go snorkeling, you might feel nervous and frightened. That's OK! A little bit of fear can make you more careful. Being careful is important when you are snorkeling. Just remember that snorkeling is not dangerous unless you are careless.

Sometimes water leaks in through the mask while you are in the water. Masks are designed so that snorkelers can easily get rid of the water.

Clearing the mask of water is something you should learn before going snorkeling. It takes a little practice at first, but it is easy to do. When the mask fills with water, take a deep breath through your snorkel, tilt your head up, pull the bottom of the mask away from your face, and exhale through your nose. The air should force the water out the bottom of the mask. Quickly push the mask back on your face.

Take a Class

Before you snorkel, it's a good idea to get training from an experienced teacher. During your training, you will get used to swimming with the mask and fins on, breathing through the snorkel, and clearing the mask of water.

Rules to Snorkel By

One of the first rules in snorkeling is never go alone. Always snorkel with a trusted adult. Snorkeling with a group of people is the safest choice. It's also a lot of fun. Groups of snorkelers can look out for one another and share stories of what they've seen in the deep.

When you get to the snorkeling site, check the condition of the weather and of the water. It can be dangerous to snorkel in stormy seas or strong waves.

Cave Creatures

Never stick your hand into a cave or a hole. Animals often hide or live in holes and may bite you.

If you are a nervous snorkeler or swimmer, be sure to use a snorkel vest. A little air in the vest will help you float facedown in the water. A lot of air in the vest will allow anyone to float comfortably at the surface.

Many underwater creatures are so beautiful you'll want to reach out and touch them. But you should never touch anything. Some creatures may bite or sting you. Even the prettiest marine creatures can be poisonous.

It's a good idea to become familiar with poisonous species. Remember that even the most dangerous sea creatures will leave you alone unless you touch or chase them.

Under the Sea

Coral reefs are popular places to snorkel. Many creatures live in or around coral reefs. These reefs are a wonder to see. The reef structure is often colorful and made up of many shapes and types of coral.

Sea grasses and algae are the most common underwater plants. Phytoplankton are microscopic plants that float in the water. Like plants on land, they make their own food by using sunlight. They are also a source of food for fish and other sea life.

Coral reef

Some flowering plants are mangroves and types of sea grasses such as turtle grass, eel grass, and surf grass.

Fish are the most common and noticeable sea creatures. Fish are cold-blooded animals that breathe under water through gills. Tropical fish are very colorful and exciting to watch.

Fish are not the only animals you will find in the ocean. You also might see mollusks, such as octopus and squid, and crustaceans, such as crabs and lobsters.

Some reptiles live in the ocean, too. Sea turtles and sea snakes are sometimes spotted by snorkelers. You might even see big sea mammals, such as seals and whales.

Sea Lizard

The marine iguana (right) is found near the Galapagos Islands. It eats algae and is the only species of marine lizard that is completely dependent on the marine environment for its food.

Look, But Don't Touch

Corals are lovely to look at but not to touch. All corals have the ability to sting. And these stings can be very painful.

Other creatures bite rather than sting. Their bites can create deep wounds. Triggerfish, pufferfish, eels, and barracuda are examples of biting marine creatures.

Some venomous underwater creatures to watch out for are the Portuguese man o' war, stingrays, sea urchins, and marine catfish.

Pufferfish

Sea urchins

Ouch!

Corals are not the only stingers in the ocean. The box jellyfish (below) —found mainly near Australia—will sting you if you get too close.

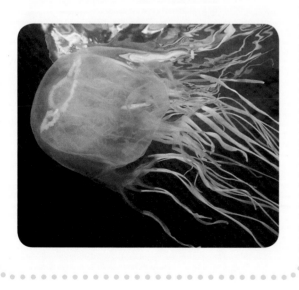

Their venom usually isn't deadly to humans if the sting is treated immediately.

Sharks are some of the most feared sea animals, but most sharks are not dangerous. Like almost all underwater creatures, if you leave sharks alone, they'll leave you alone.

Think Ahead

A bottle of drinking water is a good item to have during your snorkeling trip. Depending on how long the trip lasts, a snack or light lunch also might be a good idea.

Important First-Aid Items

- Meat tenderizer for poisonous stings
- Rubbing alcohol to clean wounds
- Vinegar for jellyfish stings
- Antihistamine for allergic reactions
- Bandages
- Cotton swabs
- Tweezers for stingers or slivers
- Soap
- Scissors

Don't forget to protect yourself from the sun. The sun's harmful rays can penetrate water. Because regular sunscreen may damage coral, wear one that contains titanium oxide or wear protective clothing. And always have a first-aid kit nearby.

Maintaining Your Equipment

If you own snorkeling gear, it's important to keep it in good working order. If it's not properly taken care of, snorkeling equipment can break or crack.

When you get out of the water, remove your gear and soak it in a freshwater rinse tank. After the items have soaked about an hour, take them out and rinse them with a hose. This will get rid of any remaining salt.

Next you should air-dry your gear. Dry it in a place that has good airflow. Hang the items so they can drip-dry. Never use wire or metal hangers. Metal or wire can rust and stain your gear.

Never put your equipment away wet. Wet gear packed in a suitcase or bag for too long can cause mildew to grow.

Rinse Cycle

A rinse tank is any large container filled with fresh water. You can use a clean, plastic garbage can or even a bathtub.

The Great Barrier Reef

Off the coast of eastern Australia lies the Great Barrier Reef. It's the largest coral reef in the world. The Great Barrier Reef is 1,250 miles (2,012 kilometers) long. It is so big it can be seen from space!

The Great Barrier Reef is made up of thousands of smaller reef formations. Coral, fish, crabs, starfish, and mollusks are some of the creatures that live in the reef. Some reef formations look like amazing

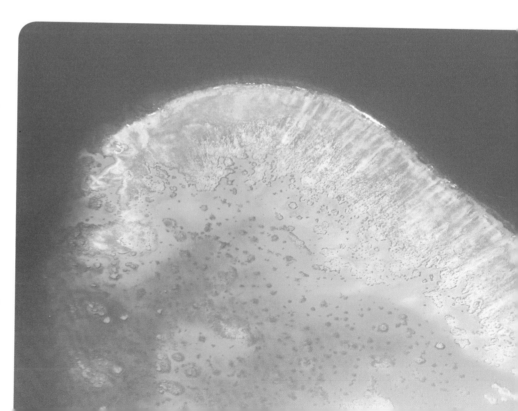

underwater gardens. They are full of unusual shapes and bright colors.

Some of the most amazing sea creatures live on or near the Great Barrier Reef. The short-tail stingray is 15 feet (4.6 meters) wide and weighs more than 1 ton (907 kilograms). Though it looks scary, the giant stingray usually isn't a threat to divers and snorkelers.

The world's largest oysters live in the Great Barrier Reef. Squid and octopus live there, too.

Friendly Fish
Scuba divers and snorkelers love to explore the Great Barrier Reef. Many fish are friendly to snorkelers and often swim around them.

Clean Water

Marine life is essential to human life. Much of the oxygen we breathe is produced by phytoplankton. The ocean's food chain is important to human survival. If ocean life dies off, humans will die, too.

Don't Litter

Trash and litter thrown from boats or along beaches are harmful to sea creatures. Fish and reptiles can be strangled by plastic bags or poisoned from bottles and liquids thrown into their home.

Pollution is threatening the world's oceans. Waste and toxic chemicals have been dumped into the water. This pollution causes marine plants and animals to die.

Never throw any trash into the ocean. If you see people littering, stop them or pick up their garbage. Any little thing you can do will help preserve the underwater world.

Fear of the Fin

Many people are afraid of sharks. Almost everyone has heard stories of shark attacks. But shark attacks are rare. You have a better chance of getting struck by lightning than being bitten by a shark.

There are more than 450 species of sharks. Only about 12 species are considered dangerous to divers and swimmers. The great white shark has the most reported fatal attacks. The tiger shark and the bull shark are also dangerous.

Most sharks are not dangerous if you leave them alone. Never chase or touch a shark. Many sharks search for food on reefs and shallow sandbars close to shore. Some shark species—such as nurse sharks, white-spotted bamboo sharks, and white-tip reef sharks— live around reefs. Bottom-dwelling sedentary sharks are not a threat and can be fun to watch.

Big Fish

The whale shark (below) is the largest fish in the ocean. It feeds on plankton and small shrimp called krill. The whale shark is not considered dangerous to humans.

Where to Go

There are thousands of places that teem with underwater life. What you wish to see will determine where you choose to snorkel. Many marine species live in the Great Barrier Reef in Australia. But you don't have to go to Australia to see something amazing. Here are a few of the great snorkeling sites around the world:

The Bahamas: The warm tropical waters around these Caribbean islands are a great place to snorkel. Sunken ships around the islands attract many snorkelers. But the greatest draw of the Bahamas is the spotted dolphin. The dolphins in this area have become comfortable with snorkelers. Often they will swim right up to you.

Florida: Florida's springs and rivers along the Gulf of Mexico are great places to see manatees. You also can enjoy year-round warm-water snorkeling at Biscayne National Park near Miami and Dry Tortugas National Park 70 miles (113 km) west of the Florida Keys. These parks are part of the third-largest coral reef system in the world.

Gentle Giants

Manatees (below) are large, gentle sea mammals. They can grow to more than 13 feet (4 m) long and weigh up to 3,500 pounds (1,588 kg). Although manatees may look gentle, it's not a good idea to get too close—they're an endangered species and are protected by state and federal laws.

Belize: This country in Central America has the largest barrier reef in the Western Hemisphere. The shallow, warm water makes the reef an excellent place to snorkel.

Indonesia: People visit this beautiful Southeast Asian country for many reasons, and snorkeling is one of them. Bunaken Island is popular with snorkelers. Hard and soft corals make up the reefs around the island. Butterfly fish, barracuda, eels, turtles, and sharks swim through the waters.

Making It Happen

Jacques Cousteau (right) was one of the first to study underwater life and photograph it for the world to see. In 1943, he helped design the air tank used in scuba diving. In the 1950s, he sailed his ship *Calypso* around the world. He and his crew dived into various oceans to film, photograph, and study marine life.

One of Cousteau's goals was to preserve the world's oceans and marine life. He wrote more than

50 books and produced 120 television programs that educated people about oceans. His films and photographs made the underwater world come alive.

Many people today help others discover the wonders of the ocean. Snorkeling tourism is a big business in many tropical lands. Tour guides and organizers help make snorkeling possible for everyone. Trained divers hold classes for beginning scuba divers and snorkelers. Experienced captains take boats of snorkelers out to sea. These captains know the best snorkeling sites. They are also familiar with the ocean's conditions and know if it's safe to snorkel. Many captains have medical training, so they know what to do in case of an emergency. These talented and trained divers and captains make snorkeling a fun and safe experience for everyone.

Snorkelers also can swim from shore in many locations. A wide variety of marine life lives along piers and docks.

What Happened When?

3000 B.C.	400 A.D.	1500	1600	1700	1800

3000 B.C. Divers use hollow reeds to help them breathe under water.

400 A.D. Xerxes, the king of Persia, employs divers for military campaigns.

1500 Leonardo da Vinci begins sketching a design for an underwater diving suit.

1869 Jules Verne writes *Twenty Thousand Leagues Under the Sea*, a novel that inspires many to explore the ocean.

333 B.C. Alexander the Great goes under water inside a diving bell, a glass cage filled with air that is lowered into the sea.

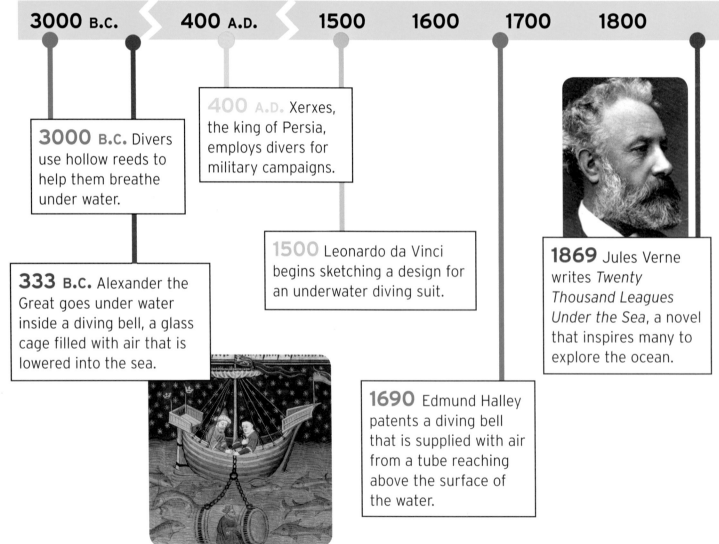

1690 Edmund Halley patents a diving bell that is supplied with air from a tube reaching above the surface of the water.

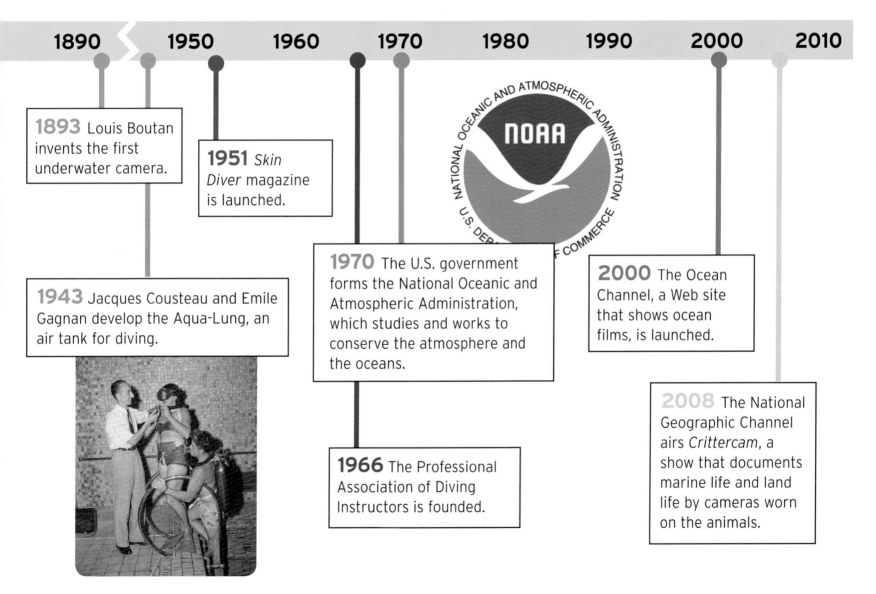

1890   1950   1960   1970   1980   1990   2000   2010

1893 Louis Boutan invents the first underwater camera.

1951 *Skin Diver* magazine is launched.

1943 Jacques Cousteau and Emile Gagnan develop the Aqua-Lung, an air tank for diving.

1970 The U.S. government forms the National Oceanic and Atmospheric Administration, which studies and works to conserve the atmosphere and the oceans.

2000 The Ocean Channel, a Web site that shows ocean films, is launched.

1966 The Professional Association of Diving Instructors is founded.

2008 The National Geographic Channel airs *Crittercam*, a show that documents marine life and land life by cameras worn on the animals.

NOAA
NATIONAL OCEANIC AND ATMOSPHERIC ADMINISTRATION
U.S. DEPARTMENT OF COMMERCE

Fun Snorkeling Facts

The Pacific Ocean is the largest and deepest ocean. It covers more than 60 billion square miles (156 billion sq km). More than 2,000 species live in the Indo-Pacific region, near Indonesia. The Indo-Pacific is a snorkeler's paradise.

Spitting on the inside of your mask can keep it from fogging up in the water. Even though it sounds gross, many experienced divers and snorkelers spit on their masks before going under water.

Some sea creatures live much longer than humans. In 2006, a 400-year-old quahog clam was found off the coast of Iceland. Sea turtles and bowhead whales can live to be more than 100 years old.

Sunken ships attract sea creatures in the same way that coral reefs do. Fish love to swim and hide in the crevices of ships. Sponges, algae, oysters, barnacles, and corals attach themselves to ship surfaces. Sunken ships are popular places for diving and snorkeling.

Underwater weddings are becoming popular among snorkelers and scuba divers. Many snorkeling tours and tropical resorts can arrange for underwater wedding ceremonies.

Snorkeling isn't the only sport you can do with a mask and a snorkel. In the 1950s, the first underwater hockey game was played in England. Underwater hockey is played much like ice hockey, except that it's played at the bottom of a pool. Players wear masks, snorkels, and fins. The puck is heavy and glides along the pool floor. Players chase the puck with hockey sticks and try to get it into the goal.

Snorkeling Words to Know

algae: small plants without leaves or stems that grow in water

cold-blooded: animals that have body temperatures that change according to the temperature of their surroundings

coral polyps: small animals that make up a coral community

coral reefs: structures made out of the skeletons and live tissue of coral polyps

crustaceans: sea animals that have outer skeletons

mammals: warm-blooded animals with backbones; female mammals produce milk for their young

marine: having to do with the sea and saltwater

mollusks: animals with soft bodies and no spines and that are usually protected by a hard shell

reptiles: cold-blooded animals that have backbones and lay eggs

schools: groups of fish or other sea creatures

scuba diving: underwater swimming with an air tank connected to a diver's mouth by a hose

snorkeling: surface swimming with a mask and a breathing tube that reaches above the water

tropical: having to do with the hot, rainy area of the tropics, the area near the equator

GLOSSARY
Other Words to Know

buoyancy: ability to stay afloat

essential: very important, necessary

microscopic: too small to be seen without a microscope

mildew: white, powdery fungus that can grow on damp materials

penetrate: go through

sedentary: not moving much

toxic: poisonous

venomous: type of animal that can inject a poisonous substance called venom

Where to Learn More

MORE BOOKS TO READ

Bailer, Darice. *Dive! Your Guide to Snorkeling, Scuba, Night-Diving, Free-Diving, Exploring Shipwrecks, Caves, and More.* Washington, D.C.: National Geographic Society, 2002.

Crockett, Jim. *The Why-To of Scuba Diving.* New York: Aquaquest Publications, 2002.

Mason, Paul. *Snorkeling and Diving.* Mankato, Minn.: Smart Apple Media, 2000.

ON THE ROAD

Snorkel Bob's Kona
75-5831 Kahakai St.
Kailua-Kona, HI 96740
808/329-0770

South Florida Diving Headquarters
101 N. Riverside Drive
Pompano Beach, FL 33062
800/771-3483

ON THE WEB

For more information on this topic, use FactHound.

1. Go to *www.facthound.com*
2. Choose your grade level.
3. Begin your search.

This book's ID number is 9780756540348

FactHound will find the best sites for you.

INDEX

air tanks, 9, 40
Australia, 32–33, 38

Bahamas, 38
Belize, Central America, 39
Biscayne National Park, 39
boat snorkeling, 15, 41
buoyancy control devices, 9

clearing the mask, 21
coral reefs, 10–11, 24, 26–27,
    32–33, 39
Cousteau, Jacques, 40–41

dangerous marine life, 23, 26–27,
    36–37
dive skins, 18–19
diving helmets, 7
dolphins, 11, 38
drinking water, 28
Dry Tortugas National Park, 39

environment, protecting the,
    34–35, 40–41
exploring the oceans, 6–7, 40–41

first-aid kit, 29
Florida, 39
free-diving, 9
freshwater snorkeling, 14–15

Galapagos Islands, 25
gear, 8, 12–13, 15, 16–19, 30–31
gear, taking care of, 30–31
Great Barrier Reef, 32–33, 38
Gulf of Mexico, 39

Indonesia, 39

jellyfish, 27, 29

learning to dive, 20–21, 41

manatees, 39
masks, 8, 12, 16–17, 21
mouthpiece, 12, 17

ocean exploration, 6–7, 14, 40–41

phytoplankton, 24, 34
places to dive, 22, 24, 38–39
poisonous water creatures, 11, 23,
    26–27
pollution, 34–35
protective clothing, 13, 18–19, 29

rinse tank, 30–31

safety precautions, 13, 26–27, 29
safety rules, 22–23
saltwater snorkeling, 14–15,
    30–31
scuba diving, 8–9, 33, 40, 41
sea snakes, 11, 25
sharks, 4, 27, 36–37, 39
shore snorkeling, 14–15, 41
Siebe, Augustus, 7
snorkel tube, 8, 12, 17
snorkel vest, 13, 23
stingrays, 26, 33
sunscreen, 29
swim fins, 13

tours and guides, 41
toxic chemicals and waste,
    34–35
training classes, 21, 41

underwater breathing, 6–7, 8,
    9, 12

water conditions, 22, 41
water pollution, 34–35
weather, 22
wet suits, 13, 18–19
whales, 4, 25

ABOUT THE AUTHOR

Jessica Gunderson grew up in North Dakota, far from the ocean. When she was 25 years old, she saw the ocean for the first time and has loved it ever since. She loves reading about shipwrecks and hopes to snorkel to a shipwreck site in the Great Lakes one day. Gunderson is a writer and teacher in Madison, Wisconsin, where she lives with her husband and cat.